Stupid EASY

CLEAN EATING RECIPES 101

Elisa C. Gwilliam MEd CHC

and

Debbie Justs CHC AADP

Stupid EASY

CLEAN EATING RECIPES 101

Balboa Press books may be ordered through booksellers or by contacting:

Balboa Press
A Division of Hay House
1663 Liberty Drive
Bloomington, IN 47403
www.balboapress.com
1 (877) 407-4847

Interior Image Credit: Mike Polito

ISBN: 978-1-9822-3745-5 (sc)
ISBN: 978-1-9822-3746-2 (e)

Library of Congress Control Number: 2019916804

Printed in the United States of America.

Balboa Press rev. date: 01/15/2020

BALBOA.PRESS
A DIVISION OF HAY HOUSE

Table of Contents

LET'S GET STARTED!

We left room for notes after each recipe
to make it your own, be creative.

Introduction

Why We Wrote This Book

After working with people in the field of health and wellness for the past decade, we noticed that many people were simply stuck eating the same foods, or confused by all the marketing - superfood today, toxin tomorrow! Together we wanted to combine our knowledge of food with our experience in the kitchen to create Supid Easy Recipes. Whether you are single or cooking for a large clan, our recipes are sure to please.

STAY HOME AND COOK

Our goal is to
> Get you in the kitchen
> Eating real food, and to
> Stop relying on processed foods

By doing this you will
> Have increased energy
> Better sleep
> Clarity over brain fog
> Balanced weight

This book will show you how to find the Healthy You!

Getting Started

Pantry

Your pantry is the heart of your kitchen. It will help you create delicious meals with limited time, ingredients and sanity. When it comes to your pantry keep it simple and invest in high quality ingredients.

The recipes in this cookbook utilize the following pantry ingredients.

Flours:
> Almond Flour
> Coconut Flour
> Oat Flour

Beans:
> Chickpeas
> Black Beans
> Pinto
> Mung (moong) Bean or
> Mung Dal
> Cannellini

Oils and Vinegars:
> Avocado Oil
> Olive Oil
> Apple Cider Vinegar
> Coconut Oil
> Sesame Oil
> Rice Vinegar

Spices:
> Pink Salt
> Pepper
> Cumin Powder
> Cumin Seeds
> Oregano
> Cinnamon
> Cayenne Pepper
> Pumpkin Pie Spice
> Ground Cloves
> Ground Nutmeg
> Dill
> Thyme
> Paprika
> Bay Leaf
> Turmeric
> Garlic Powder
> Mustard Seeds
> Crushed Red Pepper
> Flakes
> Cardamon

Coriander
Cayenne Pepper
Fennel Seeds

Sugars:
  Maple Sugar
  Honey
  Maple Syrup

Grains:
  Rice, Short Grain
  Brown
  Rice, Basmati
  Oatmeal, Steel Cut
  Oatmeal, Quick Cook
  Pasta, Brown Rice
  Rice Noodles
  Quinoa

Nuts and Seeds:
  Cashews
  Almonds
  Pecans
  Peanuts
  Pumpkin Seeds
  Hemp Seeds
  Chia Seeds
  Flax Seeds

On the shelves:
  Peanut Butter
  Bone Broth, Chicken
  Pancake Mix (we like
  Arrowroot)
  Cocoa Powder

Cranberries
Bread (we like
Mestemacher
Three Grain Bread)
Powder Sugar
Baking Soda
Baking Powder
Crushed Tomatoes,
28-ounce can
Nutritional Yeast
Soy Sauce or Coconut
Aminos
Kombu
Tahini
Panko (if possible no
sugar added)
Worchester Sauce
Mustard, Dijon
Vanilla Extract
Popcorn, white corn
kernels
Coconut Milk,
15-ounce can

Bottle of Wine ….lol

Utensils

Basics:
- Cutting Board, large wooden
- Cutting Board, plastic for meats
- Measuring Spoons and Cups (we prefer metal over plastic)
- Mixing Bowls
- Baking Sheet
- Mesh Strainer
- Tongs
- Wooden Spoon
- Silicone Spoon
- Vegetable Peeler
- Microplane Zester
- Whisk
- Kitchen Shears
- Grater
- Can Opener

Knives:
- 8 inch Chef's Knife
- 6 inch Serrated Knife
- 4 inch Paring Knife

Pots and Pans:
- 10-12 inch Skillet
- 8 Quart Stock Pot
- 2 Quart Saucepan
- Cookie Sheet
- Muffin Tins

Appliances:
- Food Processor
- Blender
- Crock Pot
- Toaster
- Mixer
- Air Popper

Other:
- Cooling Rack
- Pot Holder
- Towels
- Colander, small
- Colander, large
- Parchment Paper

Should I Buy Organic?!?!

The foods with the least pesticides are called the Clean 15, while the 12 foods with the most pesticides are called the Dirty Dozen. These lists are fantastic to reference when making your shopping list or to take with you on your shopping trips to know when to buy organic and when it's ok to buy conventional.

Clean 15	Dirty 12
1. **Avocados**	1. **Strawberries**
2. **Sweet corn**	2. **Spinach**
3. **Pineapples**	3. **Kale**
4. **Sweet peas (frozen)**	4. **Nectarines**
5. **Onions**	5. **Apples**
6. **Papayas**	6. **Grapes**
7. **Eggplants**	7. **Peaches**
8. **Asparagus**	8. **Cherries**
9. **Kiwis**	9. **Pears**
10. **Cabbage**	10. **Tomatoes**
11. **Cauliflower**	11. **Celery**
12. **Cantaloupes**	12. **Potatoes**
13. **Broccoli**	
14. **Mushrooms**	**...I also like to add Peppers**
15. **Honeydew**	**to this list.**

Let's Get Started!

Breakfast

STEEL CUT OATS WITH TOPPINGS

Prep time: 5 minutes   **Cook Time:** 30 minutes   **Total Time:** 35 minutes

Makes: 1 serving

1 cup steel cut oats   ½ cup fresh berries (use your favorite)
1 cup cashew milk   1 cup of sliced raw almonds
2 cups water   Sprinkle of cinnamon

1. Put all your ingredients into your work area and read the recipe before starting prep
2. In a pot, add oats, cashew milk, and water and bring to a boil
3. Lower to a simmer for 30 minutes, stirring occasionally so the oats do not stick to the bottom of the pan, add water if needed. Cooking for 30 minutes makes the oats become creamy
4. When done take a ½ cup serving of cooked oats and place in a bowl
5. Add your toppings. So delicious!

I add chia, flax, hemp seeds to mine. You can add whatever makes you happy.

Steel Cut Oats: Have 7 grams of protein for a ¼ cup, best part it's a complete protein. Fiber anyone? That's right 5 grams of fiber per ¼ cup.

FLORIDA OATMEAL WITH BANANAS

Assembly time: 3 minutes   *Cook Time:* 5 minutes   *Total Time:* 8 minutes

Makes: 1 serving

For the oatmeal:

1 banana, peeled
½ cup Gluten-Free old fashioned oats

1 cup water or almond milk or oat milk
1 teaspoon coconut oil

Additional topping ideas:

1 teaspoon flax seeds
1 teaspoon chia seeds
1 teaspoon cashews

1 teaspoon cranberries
1 teaspoon pumpkin seeds

1. Put all ingredients into your work area and read the recipe before beginning
2. Warm liquid in a saucepan until it begins to bubble
3. Remove liquid from heat, add oatmeal, cover for three minutes or until liquid is absorbed
4. While waiting, mash the banana in a bowl
5. Add hot oatmeal to banana, and combine
6. Stir in coconut oil and add desired toppings

My daughter loved this so much growing up in Miami!

Bananas: They are a natural way to help moderate Blood Sugar Levels, Improve Digestion, and Prevents Hypertension. Great for the whole family!

DEBBIE'S MORNING TOAST

Prep Time: 4 minutes   ***Assembly Time:*** 1 minute   ***Total Time:*** 5 minutes

Makes: 1 serving

1 slice of Mestemacher Three Grain Bread
2 tablespoons All-Natural Peanut Butter or
Almond Butter (Peanut or Almond or whatever
you prefer)

½ cup blueberries
Sprinkle of cinnamon

1. Put all your ingredients into your work area and read the recipe before beginning
2. Toast bread
3. Spread on peanut butter or almond butter
4. Sprinkle with cinnamon, add blueberries

This is really a quick and easy breakfast that helps you get your day started on the right foot.

Cracked Whole Grain Toast: Many studies have shown that eating whole grains may lower risk of heart disease, there are compounds found in whole grains like fiber, vitamin K, and antioxidants that can help lower the risk of stroke.

AVOCADO TOAST WITH PUMPKIN SEEDS AND CAYENNE PEPPER

Prep time: 3 minutes   **Assembly Time:** 2 minutes   **Total Time:** 5 minutes

Makes: 1 serving

2 pieces of bread, toasted   Pink salt and black pepper to taste
1 Hass avocado, mashed   Cayenne pepper, to taste
2 tablespoons pumpkin seeds

1. Put all your ingredients into your work area and read the recipe before beginning
2. Toast bread slices. Spread mashed avocado evenly onto the toasted bread
3. Sprinkle pumpkin seeds and spices over toast

Pumpkin Seeds: Contain omega-3 and omega-6 fatty acids, antioxidants, and fiber. This combination has benefits for both the heart and liver.

BUCKWHEAT PANCAKES WITH NUTS, BERRIES, AND CHOCOLATE

Prep time: 5 minutes   **Cook Time:** 10 minutes   **Total Time:** 15 minutes

Makes: 2 servings

1 cup Arrowhead Mills organic buckwheat mix
1 large egg, beaten
1 tablespoon coconut oil
1 tablespoon organic maple syrup

1 cup of unsweetened cashew milk (use any milk you like)
1/4 cup dark chocolate chips, 70% cocoa or higher
1/4 cup crushed raw pecans
1/2 cup fresh raspberries

1. Put all your ingredients into your work area and read the recipe before beginning
2. Follow the directions on the package for the pancake mix
3. Swap canola oil for the coconut oil and honey for the maple syrup
4. Add 1/4 of dark chocolate chips and crushed raw pecans mix all together
5. Heat the pan and add coconut oil to the pan; start making pancakes. Add the raspberries to the pancake just before you eat

Tip: Try warming the maple syrup before you add to your pancakes.

Pecans: This nut is loaded with healthy fats and antioxidants. Pecans help fight oxidative stress damage due to its high amount of antioxidants.

EGG FRITTATA

Prep time: 10 minutes   **Cook Time:** 20 minutes   **Total Time:** 30 minutes

Makes: 2 servings

1 cup sweet potatoes, roasted   ½ cup yellow onion, diced
4 large eggs, beaten   3 tablespoons of cheddar cheese (optional)
1 tablespoon cold water   2 tablespoons of avocado oil
1 cup red pepper, diced

1. Put all ingredients in your work area and read the recipe before beginning
2. Preheat oven at 350 degrees F
3. In an oven-safe pan add avocado oil, onions, red peppers and cook on medium heat for 7-10 minutes
4. While the vegetables are cooking, beat the eggs and cold water together, set aside
5. When the vegetables are done, add the roasted sweet potatoes cook until crisp
6. Add the eggs, let cook for about 5 minutes on the stove add cheese on top and transfer to the oven for about 10-15 minutes

This is a great dinner all you need to add to it is a green salad.

Eggs: Great source of high-quality protein, just make sure you are eating free-range eggs. Free-range eggs have more than double the amount of Omega 3's which is great for lowering triglycerides and cholesterol.

BREAKFAST COOKIE

Prep time: 3 minutes   **Cook Time:** 12 minutes   **Total Time:** 15 minutes

Makes: 6 servings, 2 cookies per serving

2 bananas

1 cup Gluten-Free old fashioned oats

¼ cup almond or peanut butter

¼ cup dark chocolate chips

1 tablespoon flax seeds

1 tablespoon chia seeds

¼ teaspoon pink salt

1. Put all your ingredients into your work area and read the recipe before beginning
2. Preheat oven to 350 degrees F. Line a rimmed baking sheet with parchment paper
3. In a large mixing bowl, mash the bananas. Add remaining ingredients and mix well
4. Form 12 golf ball sized cookies. Place on parchment paper and flatten slightly, if desired
5. Bake for 10-12 minutes, until golden

STORAGE TIP: Store in an airtight container in the refrigerator for up to 1 week.

Chia Seeds: Excellent source of omega-3 fatty acids, rich in antioxidants, and they provide fiber, iron, and calcium. Two tablespoons of chia seeds have almost 10 grams of fiber.

BERRY SMOOTHIE

Prep time: 2 minutes   **Cook Time:** 3 minutes   **Total Time:** 5 minutes

Makes: 1 serving

1 cup fresh spinach	2 tablespoons hemp seeds
2 cups nondairy milk of choice (almond, oat, hemp)	1 ½ cup frozen blueberries
	Cinnamon, dash
1 banana, peeled	Ice if desired

1. Put all your ingredients into your work area and read the recipe before beginning
2. Add all ingredients in a blender. Blend and serve (add more liquid or ice to create desired consistency)

Blueberries: They are rich in antioxidants which helps to prevent urinary tract infections, and provides relief from constipation! It also helps to prevent hair loss.

PEANUT BUTTER CHOCOLATE SMOOTHIE

Prep time: 2 minutes   **Cook Time:** 3 minutes   **Total Time:** 5 minutes

Makes: 1 serving

2 cups nondairy milk of choice (almond, oat, hemp)
2 bananas, peeled and frozen
½ cup plain Greek yogurt (or dairy-free alternative)

⅔ cup peanut butter
½ cup honey
½ cacao powder

1. Put all your ingredients into your work area and read the recipe before beginning
2. Add all ingredients in a blender. Blend and serve (add more liquid to create desired consistency)

Honey: Honey is a probiotic that also soothes cough, boost memory, reduces ulcers, and heals burns.

Main Dish

ROASTED CHICKPEA SALAD

Assembly time: 15 minutes   *Cook Time:* 30 minutes   *Total Time:* 45 minutes

Makes: 4 servings

For the chickpeas:

1 (15-ounce) can chickpeas, rinsed and drained   Pinch of pink salt
2 tablespoons of avocado oil

For the vegetable salad:

1 large red pepper, diced   1 large carrot, diced
1 large yellow pepper, diced   3 tablespoons parsley, chopped
2 celery stalks, diced

For the dressing:

¼ cup extra virgin olive oil

2 tablespoons fresh lemon juice

1 teaspoon dried oregano

Pink salt and black pepper to taste

1. Put all your ingredients into your work area and read the recipe before beginning
2. Preheat oven to 400 degrees F, line a cookie sheet with parchment paper
3. Pat the chickpeas dry so they roast
4. Place the dry chickpeas on the cookie sheet
5. Add avocado oil and pink salt; toss
6. Roast for 30-35 minutes
7. While the chickpeas are roasting; start cutting up the vegetables. Make sure the vegetables are finely diced (add any vegetables you want, make this your own)
8. For dressing; place all the above ingredients in a mason jar and shake well
9. In a large bowl, add roasted chickpeas, vegetables, and dressing toss

Chickpeas: They are low on the glycemic index, so they will not cause your blood sugar to spike great news for diabetics. One cup of chickpeas contains over 25% of your daily intake of iron.

GROUND TURKEY AND KALE SALAD

Prep time: 10 minutes   **Cook Time:** 25 minutes   **Total Time:** 35 minutes

Makes: 4 servings

1 pound lean ground turkey	1 bunch kale, stripped and cleaned
2 garlic cloves, minced	2 tablespoons of feta or goat cheese
1 red bell pepper, diced	1 cup cherry tomatoes, halved
2 celery stalks, diced	2 tablespoons avocado oil
2 carrots, diced	3 tablespoons extra virgin olive oil
1 onion small, chopped	1 lemon, juiced
Pinch of crushed red pepper flakes	Pink salt and black pepper to taste

1. Put all your ingredients into your work area and read the recipe before beginning
2. In a large pan, add avocado oil and heat pan
3. Add turkey, garlic, peppers, celery, carrots, onion, and a pinch of red crushed pepper flakes
4. Cook the turkey and vegetable mixture until the turkey is cooked through, about 20-25 minutes.
5. Stirring occasionally, so the mixture is crumbly
6. Dry kale, and chop
7. Place kale in a large bowl
8. Add extra virgin olive oil, lemon to the kale and massage the kale (the acid from the lemon helps breakdown the kale)
9. Add feta, pink salt, black pepper. Toss
10. Add the ground turkey mixture to the kale salad

Lemons: Vitamin C helps fight skin damage from the sun, reduces wrinkles, and has been known to kill some strains of bacteria that can cause acne.

VEGETABLE PAD THAI WITH CHICKEN

Prep time: 15 minutes   **Cook Time:** 20 minutes   **Total Time:** 35 minutes

Makes: 2 servings

For the vegetables:

2 teaspoons avocado oil
1 shallot, thinly sliced
1 carrot, julienned
1 cup red cabbage, shredded
2 cups snapped peas, ends trimmed

6 green onions, thinly sliced, white and light green parts
2 garlic cloves, minced
Pink salt to taste

For the chicken (optional):

1 pound local, organic boneless chicken, strips or cubes

2 tablespoons avocado oil
Pink salt and black pepper to taste

For the sauce:

3 tablespoons tamari
1 tablespoon maple syrup
2 teaspoons peanut butter

2 tablespoons fresh lime juice (approx. 2 limes)
4 ounces dry Asian rice noodles
¼ cup dry roasted peanuts, chopped

1. Put all your ingredients into your work area and read the recipe before beginning
2. Cook noodles per package directions
3. In a small bowl, whisk together the tamari, maple syrup, peanut butter, and lime juice. Set aside
4. Prep all vegetables
5. If adding chicken, heat oil in a skillet. Add chicken saute for five minutes or until cooked through. Remove from skillet and set aside
6. Heat the avocado oil in a skillet over medium-high heat. Add shallots and pink salt. Stir until shallots begin to become transparent (approx 3 minutes). Add cabbage, carrots, snap peas, and green onions. Saute for three more minutes. Add garlic and saute until fragrant
7. Add cooked and drained noodles to vegetable skillet. Stir to combine. Add chicken. Add sauce to the skillet and cook for two minutes
8. Add chopped peanuts to the top and serve

Red Cabbage: This vegetable helps get rid of headaches, great for eye and skin health, it is low in calories, and improves bone strength.

BUTTERNUT SQUASH AND MUSHROOM BAKE
WITH CASHEW CREAM SAUCE

Prep Time: 15 minutes   **Chill Time:** 4 hours   **Cook Time:** 20 minutes   **Total Time:** 4 hours; 35 minutes

Makes: 4 servings

For the squash:

1 (approx 2 pounds) butternut squash, peeled, seeded, and sliced into half-round slices
2 tablespoon avocado oil

1/8 teaspoon pink salt
1/8 teaspoon black pepper

For the cream sauce:

1/2 cup cashews, soaked for 4 hours and drained
3/4 cup water
1 tablespoon fresh lemon juice (about 1/2 lemon)

1 tablespoon nutritional yeast
1/2 teaspoon pink salt
1 garlic clove, minced

For the bake:

2 tablespoon avocado oil

8 ounces cremini mushrooms, sliced (about 3 cups)

1/2 onion, chopped

4 cups Swiss chard, chopped

2 garlic cloves, minced

1. Put all your ingredients into your work area and read the recipe before beginning
2. Preheat oven to 400 degrees F
3. Place butternut squash slices or cubes on a baking sheet lined with a nonstick baking mat or parchment paper. Drizzle with 2 tablespoon avocado oil. Sprinkle with pink salt and black pepper. Bake for 20-minutes, or until fork tender
4. While squash is baking, place cream sauce ingredients in a high speed blender and blend on high until smooth. Set aside
5. Heat 1 tablespoon avocado oil in a large pan. Add mushrooms and onion and cook, stirring occasionally, for about 5 minutes, or until onion is translucent and mushrooms are slightly golden
6. Add Swiss chard and garlic and cook an additional 2-3 minutes, or until chard is wilted and garlic is fragrant
7. In a small ovenproof dish (6-inch or 15-cm square or round), or in a loaf pan, make a layer of 4 butternut squash rounds (it's OK if the edges overlap a bit) or 1 cup of cubes. Cover with half of the mushroom-chard mixture and 1/3 of the cream sauce
8. Repeat with an additional layer of squash, mushroom-chard mixture and cream sauce. Finish with a final layer of squash and cream sauce
9. Bake in a 400 degrees F oven for 5 minutes, or until warmed through. Season with additional pink salt and black pepper to taste

Nutritional Yeast: Studies suggest that nutritional yeast may help protect against oxidative damage, lower cholesterol and boost immunity. Adults need about 2.4 mcg of vitamin B-12 per day. Just one-quarter of a cup of nutritional yeast provides more than seven times this amount. B12, vegan

BBQ CHICKEN RICE BOWL

Prep time: 10 minutes   **Cook Time:** 40 minutes   **Assembly Time:** 5 minutes

Total Time: 55 minutes

Makes: 4 servings

For the bowl:

1 pound chicken breasts or 2 cups shredded chicken
4 cups chicken broth or water, for cooking the chicken
1 cup uncooked brown rice
2 cups filtered water
1 1/4 cup fresh or frozen corn kernels

1 15-ounce can black beans, drained and rinsed
½ red onion, chopped
6 to 8 romaine lettuce leaves, chopped into strips
1 cup fresh salsa
1 cup shredded cheddar or Monterey jack cheese (optional)

For the sauce:

1 cup ketchup
1/2 cup tomato sauce
2 tablespoons apple cider vinegar
2 tablespoons Worcestershire sauce
1 tablespoon honey or maple syrup

3 teaspoons paprika
1/2 teaspoon granulated garlic
1/2 teaspoon pink salt
1/2 teaspoon ground cumin

In a rush? Use a high-quality BBQ sauce

Super Quick:
Use rotisserie chicken

1. Put all your ingredients into your work area and read the recipe before beginning
2. In a saucepan, mix all of the ingredients for the BBQ sauce. Heat over medium heat. When the sauce starts to bubble, reduce the heat to low and simmer for 3-5 minutes. Remove from heat and set aside
3. Place the chicken breasts in a 4-quart or larger pot with a lid and pour chicken broth over top. The chicken should be covered by about an inch; add additional broth or water if needed. Place over high heat and bring to a boil
4. Reduce heat to low, cover, and cook for 10 minutes. Check that the chicken is cooked through and registers 165 degrees F in the thickest part. Cook another few minutes if needed. Use tongs to transfer the cooked chicken breasts to a cutting board to cool briefly
5. When the chicken has cooled, shred the chicken breasts (you can use two forks)
6. Combine the rice with 1/2 teaspoon of pink salt and 2 cups of water (or enough to cover by about an inch). Bring to a simmer over medium heat, then lower the heat and cover. Cook until the rice is tender, 35 to 45 minutes (or according to package instructions)
7. Heat the corn and black beans together or separately in a pan or skillet over medium-high heat for 2 to 3 minutes
8. Assemble the bowls: Divide the rice, chicken, corn, beans, romaine lettuce, and red onion. Top with cheese, salsa, and guacamole, if using

Apple Cider Vinegar: Helps with weight loss, reduced cholesterol, lower blood sugar levels and improved symptoms of diabetes.

ZUCCHINI AND PINTO BEAN BOWL WITH CHIMICHURRI

Prep Time: 10 minutes   **Cook Time:** 15 minutes   **Total Time:** 25 minutes

Makes: 2 servings

For the beans:

1 1/2 cups cooked pinto beans, or one (15-ounce) can pinto beans, drained and rinsed
1/2 cup vegetable broth or water
1 bay leaf

1/2 teaspoon garlic powder
1/4 teaspoon pink salt
1/4 teaspoon ground cumin
1/4 teaspoon dried oregano

For the zucchini:

2 teaspoons olive oil
1/2 red onion, sliced

1 zucchini, trimmed and cut into 1/2-inch quarter moon slices

1 tablespoon nutritional yeast
1/4 teaspoon garlic powder

1/4 teaspoon pink salt

For the chimichurri sauce (makes about 1 cup):

4 tablespoons raw, shelled pumpkin seeds
1/4 cup water
1 ½ cup packed fresh cilantro (leaves and top parts of stems only), or 1 cup packed parsley if cilantro-adverse
1 teaspoon dried oregano

2 garlic clove, roughly chopped
1/2 teaspoon pink salt
3 tablespoons unseasoned rice vinegar
3 tablespoons olive oil
1 teaspoon maple syrup

To serve:

1 cup cooked brown rice
1 lime, cut in wedges

Dash of hot sauce (optional)

1. Put all your ingredients into your work area and read the recipe before beginning
2. In a medium pot over medium heat, combine beans, vegetable broth or water, bay leaf, garlic powder, 1/4 teaspoon salt, cumin, and oregano. Simmer, covered, for 15 minutes, then remove from heat and discard bay leaf. Set aside
3. While beans are cooking, in a large pan, heat olive oil over medium-high heat. Add zucchini, red onion, nutritional yeast, garlic powder, and 1/4 teaspoon salt, and cook until onion is translucent, and zucchini is softened, about 8-10 minutes. Remove from heat and set aside
4. To make chimichurri sauce, place chimichurri ingredients in a food processor fitted with the S blade, or a high-speed blender (I have used a personal blender). Blend until they're well mixed (the texture should resemble pesto)
5. To assemble bowls, place 3/4 cup of the beans over 1/2 cup of warm brown rice in a bowl and top with half of the zucchini mixture (about 1 cup), and about 1/3 cup of chimichurri sauce. Serve with lime wedges and hot sauce (if using)

Zucchini: Improves digestion and maintains eye health.

QUINOA FRIED RICE

Assembly time: 10 minutes   ***Cook Time:*** 20 minutes   ***Total Time:*** 30 minutes

Makes: 2 servings

1 cup quinoa
1 cup basmati rice
4 cups water
1 tablespoon sesame oil, plus more for serving
1 large onion, diced
1 large carrot, peeled and diced

1 1/2 cups peas, fresh or frozen
2 cloves garlic, minced
2 tablespoons low-sodium soy sauce or coconut aminos
Thinly sliced green onions, for garnish
Pink salt to taste

Optional:
Add prepared chicken or egg

Super Quick:
Use 3 cups of frozen vegetable mix

1. Put all your ingredients into your work area and read the recipe before beginning
2. In a saucepan, add quinoa, rice and water. Bring to a boil, reduce temperature to low and simmer for 20 minutes, or per package directions
3. In a large skillet over medium heat, heat oil. Add onions, carrots, and peas and cook until tender, 8 to 10 minutes. Add garlic and soy sauce and cook until fragrant, 1 minute more. Add cooked chicken or egg (optional)
4. Stir in cooked quinoa-rice and let heat through, 3 minutes
5. Drizzle with sesame oil and top with green onions

Quinoa: This super seed is gluten-free, high in protein and one of the few plant foods that contain sufficient amounts of all nine essential amino acids.

KITCHARI TRADITIONAL INDIAN DISH

Prep time: 15 minutes   **Cook Time:** 60 minutes   **Total Time:** 75 minutes

Makes: 6 servings

2 tablespoons ghee or other oil
1 teaspoon cumin seeds
1 teaspoon black mustard seeds
1 teaspoon turmeric powder or chopped root
1 tablespoon cumin powder
1 inch fresh ginger, chopped
3 cups seasonal vegetables (asparagus, zucchini, squash, greens, carrots)
½ cup split mung beans or mung dal (sometimes spelled moong)

1 cup basmati rice
6 to 8 cups water
1 piece kombu
2 teaspoons pink salt to taste
Lime, juiced
Fresh cilantro, chopped
Grated coconut
Avocado, diced

This dish normally takes over an hour to make. With this Stupid Easy version you will get to experience fine Indian food at a fraction of the time.

1. Put all your ingredients into your work area and read the recipe before beginning
2. Wash split mung beans and rice thoroughly
3. In a heavy pan, heat ghee, mustard seeds, and cumin seeds on medium heat until the mustard seeds pop
4. Add ginger and turmeric
5. Add vegetables, salt, and cumin powder. Mix well. Sauté for 5 minutes, or until vegetables are soft
6. Add rice and split mung beans. Sauté for another two minutes
7. Add water and kombu. Bring to boil
8. Reduce temperature to medium-low, cover and cook for 30 minutes. It is ready when all the water has been absorbed
9. When ready, stir in coconut flakes
10. Plate food and top with cilantro, pink salt, lime, avocado, or whatever you like!

Cumin: This traditional Indian spice is great for digestion.

BEEF BOLOGNESE

Prep time: 10 minutes   ***Cook Time:*** 1 hour, 45 minutes   ***Total Time:*** 1 hour, 55 minutes

Makes: 4 servings

3 tablespoons of olive oil or avocado oil
1 medium onion, chopped
1 large carrot, finely chopped
2 celery stalks, finely chopped
5 cloves garlic, minced
2 pounds of grass-fed ground beef

1/2 cup wine (a light white or a light rose')
1 (28-ounce) can of crushed tomatoes
1 cup chicken bone broth
1 cup unsweetened cashew milk
Pink salt a black pepper to taste

1. Put all your ingredients into your work area and read the recipe before beginning
2. In a large deep saucepan add avocado oil and all vegetables and yes garlic is a vegetable, cook over medium heat until veggies are soft (10 minutes)
3. When veggies are soft increase heat add grass fed beef cook beef thoroughly, until no longer pink (10-15 minutes)
4. Lower temperature to medium. Add wine and cook until the alcohol evaporates
5. Add crushed tomatoes and bone broth and cook until the sauce just starts to reduce (20 minutes) and lower heat to a simmer
6. Add cashew milk cook for another 30 minutes Done!

Celery: Studies show that by eating celery daily may reduce LDL, the bad cholesterol.

CHICKEN AND SPINACH MEATBALL IN SIMPLE MARINARA

Prep Time: 15 minutes   **Cook time:** 45 minutes   **Total Time:** 60 minutes

Makes: 4 servings

For the meatballs:

2 pounds ground chicken
½ cup cooked brown rice, cooled
2 tablespoons nutritional yeast
1 large egg, beaten
⅓ cup cannellini beans, puréed

1 tablespoon avocado oil
1 healthy pinch of crushed red pepper flakes
4 garlic cloves, minced
3 cups fresh spinach

For the sauce:

1 (28 ounce) can of crushed tomatoes

3 tablespoons avocado oil

7 cloves garlic, minced

4-5 big leaves of fresh basil

1 pinch of crushed red pepper flakes

1. Put all your ingredients into your work area and read the recipe before beginning
2. In a pan add avocado oil and turn heat on low, add red crushed pepper flakes, garlic and sauté until garlic is soft; add spinach
3. Cook until the spinach is wilted. Set aside and cool
4. Preheat oven to 400 degrees F
5. Line cookie sheet with parchment paper
6. In a large bowl add ground chicken, beaten egg, cooked brown rice, nutritional yeast, puréed cannellini beans,and spinach
7. Mix until incorporated try not to over mix, the mixture will be wet
8. Shape into meatballs, place on a cookie sheet lined with parchment paper
9. Baked for 30 minutes
10. In a pan add avocado oil, minced garlic, crushed red pepper flakes
11. Cook until garlic is soft
12. Add crushed tomatoes
13. Add basil
14. Let simmer for 20 minutes
15. Add cooked chicken meatballs
16. Let simmer another 20 minutes

Spinach: It's loaded with fiber! Spinach is one of the best vegetables to eat if you are suffering with constipation.

SWEET POTATO AND BLACK BEANS OVER ARUGULA
WITH GREEN GODDESS DRESSING

Prep Time: 20 minutes   **Cook Time:** 20 minutes   **Total Time:** 40 minutes

Makes: 2 servings (about 4 cups salad plus 1/4 cup dressing per serving)

For the bowl:

2 sweet potatoes, scrubbed or peeled, cubed (about 3 cups)
1 tablespoon olive oil
Pinch pink salt and black pepper
4 cups arugula

1 cup cooked black beans, drained and rinsed
1 cucumber, chopped
1 cup cherry tomatoes, halved
1/2 cup raw shelled pumpkin seeds

For the Green Goddess Dressing:

1/4 cup tahini
1/4 cup water
1 garlic clove, chopped
1 tablespoon lemon juice

1/4 teaspoon pink salt
Black pepper to taste
1/4 cup spinach, leaves only, loosely packed
3 tablespoons fresh parsley, chopped

1. Put all your ingredients into your work area and read the recipe before beginning
2. Preheat the oven to 400 degrees F. Toss the sweet potato cubes gently with olive oil, salt, and black pepper. Roast for 20 minutes, or until they're crispy on the edges and tender
3. While the potatoes roast, make the Green Goddess Dressing by blending all dressing ingredients in a high-speed blender or food processor until smooth
4. Place half the arugula in the bottom of a serving bowl. Place 1/2 cup of cooked black beans, half the sweet potato cubes, half a cucumber, and half the cherry tomatoes on top of the arugula
5. Add 1/4 cup of the Green Goddess Dressing, sprinkle with 2 tablespoons pumpkin seeds, mix ingredients together, and serve

Arugula: Helps absorb minerals, high in antioxidants, and great for your eyes and bones.

TURKEY MEATBALLS WITH HOMEMADE TOMATO SAUCE

Assembly time: 15 minutes   *Cook Time:* 35 minutes   *Total Time:* 50 minutes

Makes: 2 servings

For the meatballs:

¼ cup plain panko (no sugar added)

2 tablespoons cashew milk (use any milk you like)

1 large egg, lightly beaten (use 1 egg per pound)

½ cup grated Romano

¼ cup nutritional yeast

1 pound ground turkey (93% lean)

Pink salt and black pepper to taste

For the sauce:

2 tablespoons olive oil

1 small onion, chopped

3 cloves garlic, chopped

2 celery stalks, diced

1 large carrot, diced

Pink salt and black pepper to taste

Small pinch crushed red pepper flakes (optional)

2 (28 ounce) cans organic crushed tomatoes

1. Place all your ingredients in work area and read the recipe before starting prep.
2. Preheat oven at 400 degrees F, line a cookie sheet with parchment
3. In a large bowl add panko and milk; let the Panko absorb the milk just takes a couple of minutes
4. Add beaten egg, Romano, nutritional yeast, turkey
5. Combine gently do not overwork the meat
6. Season with pink salt and pepper
7. Shape into meatballs about the size of a golf ball, place on lined cookie sheet and bake for 30 minutes
8. In a large pot, heat oil over medium heat
9. Add onion,garlic saute until translucent (about 5 minutes)
10. Add celery, carrots pink salt and pepper to taste
11. Add pinch of red crushed pepper flakes
12. Sauté until vegetables are soft (5-10 minutes)
13. Add the crushed tomatoes; and simmer for 20 minutes
14. Add meatballs and serve

Turkey: Great source of protein! When skinless, it is low in fat. It may even help lower cholesterol.

CAULIFLOWER CHICKEN SAUSAGE OVER BROWN RICE PASTA

Prep time: 10 minutes   **Cook Time:** 45 minutes   **Total Time:** 55 minutes

Makes: 4 servings

2 pounds chicken sausage (out of casing)
5 cloves garlic, minced
4 tablespoons avocado oil
Pinch of crushed red pepper flakes
1 large head cauliflower (cleaned and broken into small pieces)

16-ounces of organic chicken bone broth
3 tablespoons of oat flour
2 tablespoons of nutritional yeast
1 pound brown rice pasta
Pink salt and black pepper to taste

1. Put all your ingredients into your work area and read the recipe before beginning
2. Preheat oven at 400 degrees F
3. Place cleaned, broken, and dried cauliflower on a cookie sheet lined with parchment paper
4. Drizzle with two tablespoons of avocado oil

5. Add pink salt to taste
6. Roast for about 30-35 minutes
7. Go in and shake the pan occasionally
8. In a large pan, add two tablespoons avocado oil and finely minced garlic
9. Add pinch of red crushed pepper flakes
10. Cook on low heat until the garlic is translucent
11. Increase heat add chicken sausage
12. Cook until the sausage is cooked through
13. Add roasted cauliflower
14. In a saucepan, bring chicken bone broth to a rapid boil
15. Add oat flour one tablespoon at a time whisking vigorously until thickened
16. Add nutritional yeast
17. Cook the brown rice pasta according to the package
18. Add pasta in the pan with cauliflower, chicken sausage
19. Add the bone broth sauce
20. Mix together

I came up with this recipe for my son, who loves sausage and roasted cauliflower.

Cauliflower: High in choline. Choline helps with brain development and making neurotransmitters that are needed for a healthy nervous system.

CHICKEN CUTLETS

Prep Time: 10 minutes   **Cook Time:** 25 minutes   **Total Time:** 35 minutes

Makes: 2 servings

4 thin chicken cutlets
1 large egg, beaten
2 tablespoons cold water
4 tablespoons avocado oil

1 cup of panko bread crumbs (no sugar added)
1 pinch of cayenne pepper
3 tablespoons parmesan cheese (optional)
Pink salt and black pepper to taste

1. Put all your ingredients into your work area and read the recipe before beginning
2. Line a cookie sheet with parchment paper and set the oven temperature to 400 degrees F
3. In one bowl, add the beaten egg with two tablespoons of cold water, add one tablespoons of avocado oil
4. In the other bowl, add panko, parmesan, cayenne pepper, pink salt, black pepper stir until well incorporated
5. Place one cutlet at a time in the egg wash than to the panko mixture press cutlet into the Panko mixture so the cutlet is covered
6. Place cutlets on the cookie sheet with parchment paper; drizzle the avocado oil on the cutlets, make sure there's oil on each
7. Bake for 15 minutes on the first side, then 10 minutes on the second side

Everyone who tries these cutlets love them. Try them!

Chicken Breast: Great source of lean, low fat protein that helps build muscles.

Salads and Sides

ASPARAGUS SALAD

Assembly time: 5 minutes   ***Cook Time:*** 5 minutes   ***Total Time:*** 10 minutes

Makes: 4-6 servings

2 pounds of asparagus, ends trimmed   1 teaspoon Dijon mustard
2 tablespoons fresh lemon juice   ¼ teaspoon dried dill
¼ cup extra virgin olive oil   Pink salt and black pepper to taste

1. Put all your ingredients into your work area and read the recipe before beginning
2. Trim and clean asparagus
3. Blanch* the asparagus for 3 minutes
4. Drain water
5. Place all other ingredients in a mason jar
6. Shake until the dressing comes together
7. Arrange the asparagus and drizzle with the lemon dressing

*Blanching is boiling the asparagus for 3 minutes, then transfer to an ice bath to stop the cooking process. By doing this your asparagus stays green and crisp-tender.

Asparagus: Is a natural diuretic due to the high levels of the amino acid asparagine. That same amino acid helps with blood flow so it will help lower blood pressure.

QUINOA AND BLACK BEAN SALAD

Prep Time: 5 minutes   *Cook Time:* 20 minutes   *Total Time:* 25 minutes

Makes: 2 servings (about 3 cups per serving)

For the salad:

½ cup dry quinoa
1 cup water
2 romaine lettuce leaves, chopped
1 cucumber, chopped

½ red onion, finely chopped
1 ½ cups black beans, cooked; or one (15-ounce)
can drain and rinsed
Pink salt to taste

For the dressing:

3 tablespoons olive oil
3 tablespoons apple cider vinegar
1 tablespoon maple syrup
2 teaspoons Dijon mustard

1 teaspoon cumin
½ teaspoon pink salt
Black pepper to taste

1. Put all your ingredients into your work area and read the recipe before beginning
2. Rinse the quinoa through a fine sieve. Place it in a medium pot with 1 cup water and a dash of salt. Bring to a boil and reduce to a simmer and cover. Simmer the quinoa for 15 minutes. Turn off the heat, fluff it with a fork
3. Add chopped vegetables and black beans to the quinoa
4. Whisk dressing ingredients together. Add to the salad, toss and enjoy!

STORAGE TIP: Leftovers will keep in an airtight container in the refrigerator for up to 3 days.

Black Beans: Known for high fiber and high protein They are anti-inflammatory, fight off cancer, and detoxify sulfates

ROASTED CAULIFLOWER

Prep time: 5 minutes   **Cook Time:** 30 minutes   **Total Time:** 35 minutes

Makes: 2 servings

1 head cauliflower, cleaned and core taken out, cut
into desired size

4 tablespoons of avocado oil
Pink salt, pinch

1. Put all your ingredients into your work area and read the recipe before beginning
2. Preheat oven to 400 degrees F
3. Make sure the cauliflower is dry
4. Place cauliflower on a cookie sheet lined with parchment paper, add avocado oil and toss so the oil is coating each piece, sprinkle with pink salt
5. Roast for about 20-30 minutes depending on how crispy you like it
6. Every 7-10 minutes go and shake the cookie sheet, you may even want to flip the pieces over so they get caramelized all over

Avocado Oil: Has a high smoke point which makes it great for cooking. This oil also helps reduce inflammation, and a great source of vitamin E.

STEAMED BROCCOLI WITH LEMON

Prep time: 5 minutes   **Cook Time:** 5 minutes   **Total Time:** 10 minutes

Makes: 2 servings

1 head of broccoli, clean and cut
1/2 fresh lemon, juice and zest
3 tablespoons extra virgin olive oil (EVOO)

1 garlic clove, minced
Pink salt and black pepper to taste

1. Put all your ingredients into your work area and read the recipe before beginning
2. Place cleaned broccoli in a large skillet add 1/2 inch of water
3. Cover skillet and turn on high and steam for 5-6 minutes. You will know broccoli is done when you can easily pierce with a fork. Remove broccoli when done and discard water
4. While the broccoli is cooking,place olive oil, garlic,and lemon juice and zest in a small mason jar shake to mix
5. Add the dressing to the broccoli add pink salt and black pepper to taste

Broccoli: Helps reduce inflammation throughout the body and may help fight against several cancers.

ROASTED BRUSSEL SPROUTS

Prep time: 5 minutes   **Cook Time:** 30 minutes   **Total Time:** 35 minutes

Makes: 4 servings

1 ½ pounds brussel sprouts, end trimmed and
yellow leaves removed
3 tablespoons avocado oil

1 teaspoon pink salt
½ teaspoon black pepper

1. Put all your ingredients into your work area and read the recipe before beginning
2. Preheat oven to 400 degrees F
3. Place all ingredients on parchment lined cookie sheet
4. Toss brussel sprouts in oil, salt and pepper
5. Roasted for 30 minutes; every 10 minutes or so shake cookie sheet to prevent burning
6. Remove from oven, adjust seasoning and serve

Brussel Sprouts: Looking to enrich your diet, start adding Brussel sprouts. Good source of protein and fiber. Fiber helps keep your digestive system running smoothly, no constipation issues here.

SIDE SALAD WITH DIJON VINAIGRETTE OR BASIC ITALIAN DRESSING

Side Salad

Prep Time: 5 minutes   ***Assembly time:*** 3 minutes   ***Total Time:*** 8 minutes

Makes: 2 servings

6 cups lettuce, Romaine or green leaf, cut to desired size
1 cucumber, peeled and diced

1 cup cherry tomatoes
1 carrot, grated

1. Place all your ingredients into your work area
2. Place lettuce in bowl and top with cucumber, tomatoes and carrot

Dijon Vinaigrette Dressing

Prep Time: 2 minutes   **Assembly time:** 3 minutes   **Total Time:** 5 minutes

Makes: 4 servings, 2 tablespoons per serving

3 tablespoons extra virgin olive oil
3 tablespoons apple cider vinegar
2 tablespoons local maple syrup

1 tablespoon Dijon mustard
2 garlic cloves, finely minced

1. Put all ingredients into your work area
2. Place all ingredients into a glass jar with a sealable lid and shake well

Basic Italian Dressing

Prep Time: 2 minutes   **Assembly time:** 3 minutes   **Total Time:** 5 minutes

Makes: 4 servings, 2 tablespoons per serving

¼ cup extra virgin olive oil
1 tablespoon apple cider vinegar
2 tablespoons lemon juice
1 tablespoon local maple syrup
1 garlic clove, finely minced
½ shallot, finely minced

1 teaspoon dried oregano
½ teaspoon crushed thyme
¼ teaspoon pink salt
Black pepper, to taste
Crushed red pepper flakes, dash

1. Place all your ingredients into your work area
2. Put all ingredients into a glass jar with a sealable lid and shake well

STORAGE TIP: Dressing will keep in an airtight container in the refrigerator for up to 1 week.

Mustard: Any kind you choose is rich in selenium, which is a must for thyroid function.

SWEET POTATO FRIES

Prep time: 5 minutes   **Cook Time:** 20 minutes   **Total Time:** 25 minutes

Makes: 4 servings

2 sweet potatoes, peeled and cut into the desired shape

2 tablespoons avocado oil
Pink salt to taste

1. Place all your ingredients into your work area and read the recipe before starting prep
2. Heat oven to 350 degrees F
3. Place sweet potato pieces on a cookie sheet in a single layer
4. Sprinkle with oil and salt
5. Bake for 10 minutes, turn over and continue baking for 10 minutes

Sweet Potatoes: Sweet potatoes are a great source of fiber, vitamins, and minerals. Contain vitamin B6, potassium, and iron which your body needs to help you grow strong. Sweet potatoes are a good source of dietary fiber which helps to promote a healthy digestive tract. Sweet potatoes have more fiber than oatmeal! Sweet potatoes are not potatoes!

RED CABBAGE CARROT SALAD WITH LIME-CUMIN DRESSING

Prep Time: 5 minutes   ***Assembly time:*** 10 minutes   ***Total Time:*** 15 minutes

Makes: 6 servings

For the salad:

1 small head red cabbage, cored and thinly sliced   1 small red onion, thinly sliced
1 large carrot, grated   1 red pepper, thinly sliced

For the dressing:

½ cup extra virgin olive oil   2 tablespoons local maple syrup
¼ cup lime juice, approximately 2-3 limes   Pink salt and black pepper to taste
1 teaspoon ground cumin

1. Put all your ingredients into your work area and read the recipe before beginning
2. In a large bowl, add all prepared vegetables
3. Add all remaining ingredients into a mason jar and shake
4. Pour over vegetables, toss

Red Onions: Have a great source of chromium a trace mineral that helps lower blood glucose levels, and are low on the glycemic index.

WARM SWISS CHARD WITH ROASTED CHICKPEAS

Prep Time: 10 minutes   **Cook Time:** 30 minutes   **Total Time:** 40 minutes

Makes: 4-6 servings

1 bunch of Swiss chard, cleaned, dried and chopped
1 medium red onion, diced and chopped

1 (15-ounce) can organic chickpeas, drained and rinsed (pat dry before roasting)
5 tablespoons avocado oil

1. Put all your ingredients into your work area and read the recipe before beginning
2. Preheat oven to 400 degrees F
3. Place chickpeas on a cookie sheet lined with parchment paper; drizzle with 3 tablespoons of avocado oil, and sprinkle with pink salt
4. Roast for 30-35 minutes; shake pan to ensure all chickpeas are getting roasted
5. While the chickpeas are roasting, cook the red onion in two tablespoons of avocado oil, cook until translucent
6. Add the chopped swiss chard to the red onions. Cook until leaves are slightly wilted
7. When chickpeas are done add to the swiss chard and red onion mixture
8. Pink salt and pepper to taste

This is a perfect side dish or a complete meal. Here's the best part it's stupid easy.

> **Swiss Chard:** Helps with brain power! Rich in potassium and vitamin K which is needed for mental development.

Snacks

KALE CHIPS

Assembly time: 5 minutes   ***Cook Time:*** 15 minutes   ***Total Time:*** 20 minutes

Makes: 4 servings

2 pounds kale, torn in desired size pieces   Pink salt to taste
⅓ cup avocado oil

1. Put all your ingredients into your work area and read the recipe before beginning
2. Preheat oven to 250 degrees F
3. Break kale into pieces, removing the stem
4. Place kale in a bowl and massage with avocado oil
5. On a cookie sheet, place kale down in a single layer, sprinkle with pink salt
6. Bake for 8 minutes, flip pieces. Bake on the other side for 7 minutes

Kale: 10x more Vit C than spinach. Low in calories, fat and carbs. Help keep skin and hair healthy and strong.

ENERGY BALLS

Prep time: 5 minutes   **Wait Time:** 30 minutes   **Total Time:** 35 minutes

Makes: 5 servings

1 cup raw almonds

¼ teaspoon pink salt

1 cup Medjool dates, pitted and tightly packed

¼ teaspoon cardamom

½ teaspoon vanilla extract

1 tablespoon cacao powder

1. Put all your ingredients into your work area and read the recipe before beginning
2. In a food processor or high-speed blender, place almonds and salt. Process or blend until nuts a roughly ground. Set aside
3. Place Medjool dates, vanilla extract, cardamom, cocoa powder in a food processor or high-speed blender. Process or blend until it is a smooth consistency
4. Remove from processor or blender and combine with almonds
5. With wet hands, knead the mixture together until it is the desired consistency. If it is crumbly, add a teaspoon of water
6. Roll into balls
7. Refrigerate for 30 minutes, serve!

Medjool Dates: They are a Fat-Free and Cholesterol-Free food. Dates help to reduce night blindness and promote healthy bowels.

HEALTHY PUMPKIN MUFFINS

Assembly time: 10 minutes   ***Cook Time:*** 30 minutes   ***Total Time:*** 40 minutes

Makes: 10-12 servings

1 ½ cups whole grain oat flour
1 teaspoon baking powder
½ teaspoon baking soda
½ teaspoon pink salt
1 teaspoon pumpkin pie spice
½ teaspoon ground cloves

½ teaspoon ground nutmeg
1 (15-ounce) can solid pumpkin
⅓ cup coconut oil (melted)
2 large eggs
1 cup maple sugar
2 tablespoons of coconut oil

1. Put all your ingredients into your work area and read the recipe before beginning
2. Grease muffin tins with coconut oil
3. In a medium size bowl whisk together oat flour, baking powder, baking soda, pink salt, pumpkin spice, cloves, and nutmeg
4. In a large bowl add pumpkin,coconut oil, eggs mix on medium speed
5. Add maple sugar mix until smooth
6. Add all dry ingredients mix until blended
7. Divide batter among muffin tins ¾ full
8. Bake at 350 degrees F until golden, approximately 25-30 minutes

Pumpkin: Helps strengthens the immune system and helps protect the eyes from blindness.

AIR POPPED POPCORN

Assembly time: 3 minutes   ***Cook Time:*** 7 minutes   ***Total Time:*** 10 minutes

Makes: 2 servings

¼ cup white corn kernels   Pink salt to taste
2 tablespoons avocado oil   Hot Air Popcorn Machine

1. Put all your ingredients into your work area and read the recipe before beginning
2. Heat up popcorn machine for a few seconds
3. Add ¼ cup corn kernels
4. Let pop into a big bowl
5. Drizzle with avocado oil
6. Toss and sprinkle with pink salt

Pop Corn: High in fiber, and low in calories. Buy organic and non-gmo.

KETTLE CORN

Prep time: 5 minutes   **Cook Time:** 5 minutes   **Total Time:** 10 minutes

Makes: 2 servings

¼ cup white corn kernels

¼ cup local maple syrup

2 tablespoons maple sugar

3 tablespoons avocado oil

Pink salt to taste

Hot Air Popcorn Machine

1. Put all your ingredients into your work area and read the recipe before beginning
2. Plug in the popcorn machine for a few minutes to heat up
3. Add corn kernels, let pop into a large bowl
4. While the corn is popping, in a small saucepan add maple syrup, maple sugar, and avocado oil
5. Cook on medium-high heat until mixture becomes bubbly
6. Pour over popcorn, sprinkle with pink salt

HUMMUS WITH VEGGIES

Prep Time: 5 minutes   *Assembly Time:* 3 minutes   *Total Time:* 8 minutes

Makes: 4 servings

For the hummus:

2 cups canned chickpeas, drained
3 tablespoons of Tahini
1 lemon, juiced
1 teaspoon ground cumin

1 teaspoon ground coriander
½ teaspoon cayenne pepper
½ cup extra virgin olive oil
Pink salt and black pepper to taste

Fresh vegetables for dipping:

Carrots
Red peppers
Celery

Kohlrabi
Radishes

1. Put all your ingredients into your work area and read the recipe before beginning
2. In a blender, combine all ingredients and blend
3. Flavor with pink salt and pepper to taste
4. Transfer to a bowl, make a small well in the middle to fill with a splash of olive oil
5. Serve with fresh vegetables

COOKING TIP: remove chickpea skins for a creamy hummus

Chickpeas: The choline in chickpeas helps with sleep, muscle movement, learning and memory.

AFTERNOON HIKE PROTEIN COOKIE

Prep time: 5 minutes   ***Cook Time:*** 10 minutes   ***Total Time:*** 15 minutes

Makes: 6 servings, 2 cookies per serving

2 bananas
1 cup Gluten-Free old fashioned oats
¼ cup almond or peanut butter
¼ cup dark chocolate chips

¼ cup dried cranberries
1 tablespoon flax seeds
1 tablespoon of chia seeds
¼ teaspoon pink salt

1. Put all your ingredients into your work area and read the recipe before beginning
2. Preheat oven to 350 degrees F.
3. Line a rimmed baking sheet with parchment paper
4. In a large mixing bowl, mash the bananas. Add remaining ingredients and mix well
5. Form 12 golf ball sized cookies. Place on parchment paper and flatten slightly, if desired
6. Bake for 10-12 minutes until golden

STORAGE TIP: Store in an airtight container in the refrigerator for up to 1 week.

Almond Butter: More protein than peanut butter. Lowers the risk of heart attack. Alkalizes the body

APPLE WITH HOMEMADE PEANUT BUTTER

Prep time: 3 minutes   **Cook Time:** 5 minutes   **Total Time:** 8 minutes

Makes: 2 serving

1 cup peanuts, shelled   2 apples, cored and cut into wedges

1. Put all your ingredients into your work area and read the recipe before beginning
2. Place peanuts in a high power blender. Blend as needed until desired consistency
3. Place in a bowl and serve with apple wedges

This recipe can also be made by using soaked almonds, or honey roasted peanuts.

Apples: Brightens the skin, reduces puffy eyes, acts as a natural toner, helps reduce acne and blemishes. Promotes smooth bowel movements.

LEMON BERRY YOGURT MUFFIN

Prep time: 10 minutes   ***Cook Time:*** 30 minutes   ***Total Time:*** 40 minutes

Makes: 10-12 servings

1 ½ cups whole grain oat flour
1 teaspoon baking powder
½ teaspoon baking soda
½ teaspoon pink salt
10 ounces plain Greek yogurt
⅓ cup coconut oil (melted)

2 large eggs
1 lemon, juice and zest
1 cup any berry
1 cup maple sugar
2 tablespoons of coconut oil

1. Put all your ingredients into your work area and read the recipe before beginning
2. Preheat oven to 350 degrees F
3. Grease muffin tins with coconut oil (for easy removal)
4. In a medium size bowl, whisk all dry ingredients
5. In a large bowl, add yogurt, lemon juice and zest, coconut oil, eggs, beat on medium speed until blended
6. Add maple sugar, blend until smooth
7. Add dry ingredients, mix until combined
8. Divide batter among muffin tins, filling each tin ¾ full
9. Bake until golden, 25-30 minutes

Oat Flour: Contains Beta-Glucan which is a soluble fiber and once it hits the gut it's a jelly like solution. This fiber helps reduce LDL (the bad cholesterol), reduce blood sugar, and helps the growth of healthy gut bacteria.

Treats without the Tricks

BERRIES WITH COCONUT WHIP CREAM

Prep time: 5 minutes   ***Wait Time:*** 24 hours; 10 minutes   ***Total Time:*** 24 hours; 15 minutes

Makes: 4 servings

1 (14-ounce) can coconut milk (full-fat)   1/4 cup and 2 tablespoons powdered sugar

1. Put all ingredients into your work area and read the recipe before beginning
2. Place the coconut milk (in the can) along with the mixing bowl and whisk attachment from a standing mixer in the refrigerator for 8 hours or overnight
3. Working quickly is key to keep your ingredients from getting warm. Assemble mixer
4. Puncture the coconut milk can with the pointed end of a can opener and drain and discard the liquid from the cans
5. Once the liquid is drained, open the can and scoop out the coconut fat from the can into the chilled mixing bowl
6. Whip the coconut fat on high speed for about 15 to 20 seconds, or until just smooth
7. Add the powdered sugar and mix for about 20 seconds more, starting at a low and quickly moving up to high, or just until incorporated. (Do not over-mix!)
8. Use vegan whipped cream immediately or store in the refrigerator for up to 3 to 4 hours before use

Berries: High in fiber and antioxidants

CHOCOLATE COCONUT ICE CREAM

Prep time: 5 minutes   **Wait Time:** 24 hours; 30 minutes   **Total Time:** 24 hours; 35 minutes

Makes: 2 servings

1 cup cashews (soaked overnight in water)   ½ cup maple syrup
1 cup coconut milk   3 tablespoons cacao powder
1 cup shredded coconut   1 tablespoon vanilla extract
4 cups mixed berries

1. Put all your ingredients into your work area and read the recipe before beginning
2. Combine all ingredients in a high speed blender. Blend until smooth
3. Place ice cream mixture into a freezer safe bowl and then into the freezer to set, stirring occasionally
4. Allow to set and eat with minimal guilt

It's free from dairy, refined sugar, preservatives and other unnecessary additives. When you make it at home, you know exactly what's going in it. Plus it's quick and easy to make, and won't cost you a fortune. It's a naughty little treat without the naughty!

Dark Chocolate: Dark chocolate is rich in minerals, such as iron, magnesium, and zinc. The cocoa in dark chocolate also contains antioxidants called flavonoids, which may provide several health benefits.

CHOCOLATE CHIA DIPPED BANANAS

Assembly time: 5 minutes   ***Wait Time:*** 30 minutes   ***Total Time:*** 35 minutes

Makes: 4 servings

5 bananas, peeled   ⅛ cup water
3 tablespoons raw cacao   2 tablespoons chia seeds
2 tablespoons maple syrup   2 tablespoons hemp seeds

1. Put all your ingredients into your work area and read the recipe before beginning
2. Insert popsicle sticks into four of the bananas. Transfer to freezer until frozen
3. Place remaining banana, cacao, maple syrup, and water in blender
4. Blend on high for 30 seconds or until smooth
5. Dip each of the frozen bananas in sauce and then sprinkle with chia and hemp seeds

Chia Seeds: Despite their small size, chia seeds are full of important nutrients. They are an excellent source of omega-3 fatty acids, rich in antioxidants, and they provide fiber, iron, and calcium. Omega-3 fatty acids help raise HDL cholesterol, the "good" cholesterol that protects against heart attack and stroke.

Beverages

INFUSED WATER

Prep time: 5 minutes   *Total Time:* 5 minutes

Makes: 8 servings

60 ounces of cold water   Fresh herbs (again any kind)
Fruit (any kind will do)

1. Put all your ingredients into your work area and read the recipe before beginning
2. In two large mason jars add the fruit and herbs, my favorite is raspberry and mint, be creative.
3. Add water to the mason jars, muddle the fruit
4. Cover mason jar and place in the refrigerator overnight

They last up to a week in the refrigerator. We all need to drink water, this is so delicious you will want to get all your water in.

Other Favorites

- Mint
- Watermelon and Basil
- Orange and water make sure to remove the rind
- Apple Carrot Lemon
- Strawberry Mint Lemon
- Peach Plum Mint
- Apple Cinnamon Stick Pear

Water: Because blood is made of 90% water, it delivers oxygen in the body. When you're dehydrated your prone to premature wrinkles, so drink your water.

DIGESTIVE TEA

Cook Time: 5 minutes   **Wait Time:** 15 minutes   **Total Time:** 20 minutes

Makes: 2 servings

4 cups water   1 teaspoon coriander seeds
1 teaspoon fennel seeds   1 teaspoon cumin seeds

1. Put all your ingredients into your work area and read the recipe before beginning
2. Place all ingredients in a pot and bring to a simmer
3. Remove from heat and let stand for 15 minutes
4. Discard seeds and store tea in a thermos or refrigerator
5. Sip on throughout the day

Fennel Seeds: Fennel tea may aid healthy digestion, and treat bloating, gas, or cramps, and may also act as a diuretic.

MORNING DETOX TEA

Liver Flush Tea

Cook Time: 5 minutes   **Total Time:** 5 minutes

Makes: 1 serving

Take 1 to 2 cups in the morning

1 cup water   Squeeze of lemon
1 inch of thinly sliced ginger   1 teaspoon local honey

1. Put all your ingredients into your work area and read the recipe before beginning
2. Bring water to a boil
3. Pour water into a mug and add remaining ingredients (added when water is lower than 180 degrees)

Lemons: This acid food is actually alkalizing for your body helps to freshen breath and is also known for preventing kidney stones.

GINGER WATER TEA

Prep time: 2 minutes   ***Cook Time:*** 10 minutes   ***Total Time:*** 12 minutes

Makes: 2 servings

80 ounces water   2 inch pieces of fresh ginger, peeled

1. Put all your ingredients into your work area and read the recipe before beginning
2. In a pot, add water and fresh ginger
3. Bring to a boil, once the water and ginger have come to a boil take off heat
4. Let steep for 10-15 minutes
5. Cool and transfer to a large glass pitcher, and place in the fridge

Ginger: A powerful anti-inflammatory that helps with nausea, especially beneficial for women going through morning sickness.

About the Authors

Elisa C. Gwilliam

A problem-solver with a passion for helping busy people find their zest for life through a healthy diet, lifestyle and mindset, Elisa believes healthy doesn't need to be complicated, time-consuming or boring.

Debbie Justs

Debbie's lifelong passion is food, cooking, and how it results in weight loss and a healthy, happier life. For over 30 years, Debbie's clients have been wanting her to write a cookbook to help them along their weight lose journey.